THE CROCKPOT COOKBOOK

Crock Pot Recipes with Pictures For Easy & Delicious Slow Cooking Meals

Kaitlyn Donnelly

CONTENTS

INTRODUCTION

When you open the front door of your home on a cold winter evening, and you smell the tempting odor of meat stew or chicken soup coming from the crock pot in the kitchen, you realize that dreams of supper are coming true. But not only is winter the right time for cooking with the crock pot but also in summer, using this small device, you can avoid the additional heat coming from the heated oven. At any time of the year, the crock pot can make life a little more convenient because of the possibility of scheduling your time. Besides, it is more economical than an electric oven.

WHAT IS A CROCK POT?

A slow cooker or a Crock Pot trademark is a counter top electric device for slow cooking at temperatures from 168° F to 284° F. Low temperatures and long cooking times allow the use of cheaper cuts of meat for stewing.

HOW DOES A CROCK POT WORK?

Many crock pot models have a ceramic inner liner, and the heating elements are located on the walls of the pan, so the heating is available to the entire volume of food being cooked. There are also two heat regulators - low and high.

WHAT ARE THE BENEFITS OF A CROCK POT?

- Increased cooking time allows better development and mixing of food flavors.
- Low temperatures reduce the possibility of burning on the bottom of a pan.
- It frees the oven for many other dishes and is quite suitable for large parties and festive meals.
- It also frees up your time for cooking other dishes.

TIPS AND TRICKS FOR USING A CROCK POT.

- For a more even process, always cut the products into small pieces.
- Fill the crock pot from ½ to ⅔ of its volume. Vegetables are prepared slower than meat and poultry, so first, put the vegetables on the bottom and along the walls of the pan. Then put in the meat and pour in the liquid contents — broth, water, or the required sauce. Do not open the lid frequently: only to stop cooking or check for degree of doneness, and occasionally to add ingredients.
- The food will be cooked faster in high mode, but if you plan to leave the pot for a whole day, set the mode to low.
- The timer on the crock pot allows you to complete the preparation of the dish, even if you are absent, but you should remember that the food should not be in the crock pot for more than two hours after being cooked, and poultry dishes not for more than one hour. It is not recommended to use the crock pot for rewarming food.
- Try not to season during cooking because a crock pot slowly develops the flavor during cooking. All seasonings — salt, pepper, spices, herbs — should be put in toward the end of the cooking time.

WESTERN OMELET CASSEROLE

SERVINGS: 4 | PREP TIME: 10 min. | COOK TIME: 10-12 h.

CARBS: 29 g | FAT: 24 g | PROTEIN: 26 g | CALORIES: 431

INGREDIENTS

- 32 oz. frozen hash brown potatoes
- 1 lb of bacon diced, crumbled
- 1 onion, diced
- 1 green bell pepper, diced
- 1½ cups Cheddar or Monterey Jack cheese, shredded
- 1 dozen eggs
- 1 cup milk
- 1 tsp salt
- 1 tsp pepper (more or less to taste)

DIRECTIONS

1. In layers place frozen potatoes on the bottom of a crock pot, followed by bacon, onions, green pepper and cheese.
2. Make two or three more layers ending with cheese.
3. Blend the eggs, milk, salt and pepper together.
4. Pour the mixture into the crock pot, cover the lid and turn on low.
5. Cook for 10-12 hours.

EASY HOT CEREAL

SERVINGS: 4-5 | PREP TIME: 10 min. | COOK TIME: 7-9 h.

CARBS: 37 g | FAT: 2.5 g | PROTEIN: 6 g | CALORIES: 190

INGREDIENTS

- ¼ cup cracked wheat
- ¼ cup steel cut oats
- ¼ cup coconut, sweetened or unsweetened
- 3 cups water
- ¼ tsp salt, or to taste
- ¼ cup pearl barley
- ¼ cup brown rice
- ½ cup of light cream or half-and-half
- ¼ cup dried cranberries

DIRECTIONS

1. Combine all ingredients except cream or half-and-half in a crock pot.
2. Cover and cook on low for 7 to 9 hours.
3. Add ½ cup of light cream and cook for another 10 minutes.
4. Garnish with some cinnamon sugar or dried cranberries. Serve with milk.

TENDER PARMESAN BASIL BISCUITS

SERVINGS: 8 | PREP TIME: 10 min. | COOK TIME: 25 min.

CARBS: 13 g | FAT: 6 g | PROTEIN: 3 g | CALORIES: 120

INGREDIENTS

- 1 cup all-purpose flour
- 1 tsp baking powder
- ¼ tsp baking soda
- ¼ tsp salt
- 3 Tbsp cold butter
- ¼ cup Parmesan cheeseб grated
- 2 Tbsp fresh basil leaves, chopped
- ½ cup buttermilk
- Cooking spray
- 1 Tbsp Parmesan cheese, shredded

DIRECTIONS

1. Heat a crock pot to 425° F. Grease a baking sheet with cooking spray.
2. In a separate bowl mix flour, baking powder, baking soda, salt and cut butter.
3. Using a blender make the smooth mixture. Stir in grated Parmesan cheese and basil. Add buttermilk, stirring constantly.
4. Make 8 equal balls out of the dough. Place onto the cookie sheet. Apply the cooking spray and shredded Parmesan cheese on the biscuits.
5. Bake in the crock pot for 10 to 12 minutes until golden.

BREAKFAST COBBLER

SERVINGS: 4 | PREP TIME: 15 min. | COOK TIME: 5-7 h.

CARBS: 25 g | FAT: 5 g | PROTEIN: 2.5 g | CALORIES: 149

INGREDIENTS

- *3 cups peeled, sliced tart apples*
- *1 tsp cinnamon*
- *2 cups granola cereal*
- *¼ cup honey*
- *3 Tbsp melted butter*

DIRECTIONS

1. Grease the inside of a crock pot with nonstick cooking spray.
2. Put the apples into the crock pot and sprinkle with the cinnamon and granola.
3. In a separate bowl stir together the honey and butter. Sprinkle over the apple mixture. Mix everything together gently.
4. Cover the crock pot and cook on low for 5 to 7 hours. Check for doneness with a fork.
5. Serve with fruit, yogurt or ice cream, if desired.

FRUITY OATMEAL

SERVINGS: 1 | PREP TIME: 20 min. | COOK TIME: 5-7 h.

CARBS: 33 g | FAT: 8 g | PROTEIN: 8 g | CALORIES: 200

INGREDIENTS

- 2 cups whole or 2% milk
- ¼ cup brown sugar
- 2 Tbsp honey
- 2 Tbsp melted butter
- ¼ tsp salt
- ½ tsp cinnamon
- 1 cup steel cut or regular oats
- 1 cup apples, peeled, chopped
- ½ cup dates, raisins, chopped
- ½ cup nuts to your liking, chopped

DIRECTIONS

1. Grease the inside of a crock pot with nonstick cooking spray.
2. Combine milk, brown sugar, honey, melted butter, salt, and cinnamon in the crock pot and mix well.
3. Mix in the oats, apples, dates or raisins, and the nuts.
4. Cover the crock pot and turn on low setting.
5. Cook 5-7 hours until oatmeal is tender. Stir well before serving.

SOUTHWEST CROCK POT BREAKFAST

SERVINGS: 12 | PREP TIME: 20 min. | COOK TIME: 7-8 h.

CARBS: 3 g | FAT: 26 g | PROTEIN: 23 g | CALORIES: 341

INGREDIENTS

- 1 Tbsp butter
- 1 lb breakfast sausage, cooked and drained
- 1 onion, chopped
- 1 green bell pepper, chopped
- 4 oz green chilies, chopped and drained
- 2½ cups Monterey Jack cheese, grated
- 18 eggs
- sour cream (optional)
- salsa (optional)

DIRECTIONS

1. Grease inside of a crock pot with butter. In layers place first the sausage, then onions, peppers, chilies, and cheese.
2. Repeat the layering process with the remaining amount of ingredients.
3. In a large mixing bowl, beat eggs with a wire whisk or an eggbeater until combined, and then pour over mixture in the crock pot.
4. Cover and cook on low 7-8 hours.
5. Serve with sour cream if desired.

EASY BREAKFAST PIE

SERVINGS: 4-6 | PREP TIME: 10 min. | COOK TIME: 6-8 h.

CARBS: 21 g | FAT: 18 g | PROTEIN: 15 g | CALORIES: 300

INGREDIENTS

- *8 eggs, whisked*
- *1 sweet potato or yam, shredded*
- *1 lb pork breakfast sausage, broken up*
- *1 yellow onion, diced*
- *1 Tbsp garlic powder*
- *2 tsp dried basil*
- *salt and pepper, to taste.*
- *any extra veggies you want to put in there: peppers, squash, etc*

DIRECTIONS

1. Grease a crock pot with a bit of coconut oil to make sure none of the egg sticks to it.
2. Shred the sweet potato.
3. Add all the ingredients into the crock pot and use a spoon to mix well.
4. Cook it on low for 6-8 hours to make sure the pork sausage is
5. completely cooked through.
6. Slice it like a pie.

CHICKEN NOODLE SOUP

SERVINGS: 6 | PREP TIME: 10 min. | COOK TIME: 30 min.

CARBS: 32 g | FAT: 8 g | PROTEIN: 24 g | CALORIES: 304

INGREDIENTS

- 2 tsp butter
- 1 cup sliced celery
- 1 cup chopped carrots
- ½ cup chopped onion
- ½ tsp thyme
- 1 tsp poultry seasoning
- 2 (32-ounce) containers plus one 14 oz can of chicken broth
- 2 tsp chicken bouillon granules
- 8 oz egg noodles
- 2 cups cooked chicken (3 frozen breasts)
- Parsley

DIRECTIONS

1. Melt butter in a crock pot.
2. Sauté the celery, carrots and onion for 5 to 10 minutes.
3. Add thyme, poultry seasoning, chicken broth and bouillon.
4. Bring to a boil.
5. Fill in noodles and chicken, and cook on low for 20 minutes.
6. Sprinkle with parsley.

BOURBON CHICKEN

SERVINGS: 2 | PREP TIME: 10 min. | COOK TIME: 3-7 h.

CARBS: 10 g | FAT: 0 g | PROTEIN: 4 g | CALORIES: 30

INGREDIENTS

- *3 lb boneless, skinless chicken thighs*
- *3 Tbsp cornstarch*
- *¼ cup sliced green onions (or more to taste)*

Sauce:
- *½ tsp fresh grated ginger*
- *4 cloves garlic, minced*
- *½ tsp crushed red chili flakes*
- *⅓ cup apple juice*
- *1½ Tbsp honey*
- *¼ cup brown sugar*
- *¼ cup ketchup*
- *3 Tbsp cider vinegar*
- *¼ cup water*
- *¼ cup Bourbon*
- *¼ cup soy sauce*
- *salt and pepper to taste*

DIRECTIONS

1. In a separate bowl mix all sauce ingredients.
2. Place chicken in a crock pot and pour the sauce over the top. Cover and cook on low for 6-7 hours or on high for 3 hours.
3. Remove chicken and chop into bite sized pieces, and cover to keep warm.
4. Meanwhile, combine 3 Tbsp water with the cornstarch. Turn the crock pot up to high. Whisk cornstarch goop into the sauce. Cover and allow to thicken. Return chicken back into the sauce and add the green onions.
5. Serve over rice.

HONEY MUSTARD PORK ROAST

SERVINGS: 8 | PREP TIME: 10 min. | COOK TIME: 7-8 h.

CARBS: 23 g | FAT: 10 g | PROTEIN: 16 g | CALORIES: 250

INGREDIENTS

- *1 onion, chopped*
- *4 cloves garlic, minced*
- *⅓ cup honey mustard*
- *1 tsp salt*
- *¼ tsp pepper*
- *1 tsp dried thyme*
- *3-lb pork roast*
- *¼ cup chicken broth*
- *1 Tbsp cornstarch*
- *¼ cup water*

DIRECTIONS

1. Grease a crock pot with nonstick cooking spray and add onions and garlic.
2. Rub salt and pepper and honey mustard over the pork roast. Sprinkle with thyme.
3. Place coated roast on top of onions and garlic. Pour the chicken broth. Cover the crock pot and cook on low for 7–8 hours.
4. Remove roast and cover with foil while making the sauce.
5. Combine the cornstarch and water in a medium saucepan and blend with a wire whisk.
6. Add juices from the crock pot and the cooked onions and garlic to the saucepan. Cook over medium heat, stirring. Remove the heat when the mixture thickens.
7. Season to taste. Add more salt, pepper, thyme, or honey mustard if needed. A crock pot mutes these flavors because of its long cooking time.
8. Slice the roast and serve it with the sauce.

TENDER PORK AND POTATOES

SERVINGS: 6 | PREP TIME: 15 min. | COOK TIME: 7-8 h.

CARBS: 62 g | FAT: 32 g | PROTEIN: 59 g | CALORIES: 596

INGREDIENTS

- *1 lb small red potatoes, cut in half*
- *1 lb sweet potatoes, peeled and cut into chunks*
- *2 red bell peppers, cut into large pieces*
- *1 (3-lb) boneless pork loin roast*
- *¼ cup Dijon mustard*
- *1 tsp dried thyme*
- *½ tsp salt*
- *⅛ tsp black pepper*
- *1½ cups low sodium beef broth*

DIRECTIONS

1. Place potatoes and bell peppers in the bottom of a 4-5 quart crock pot.
2. In a small bowl, mix mustard, thyme, salt, and black pepper and spread evenly over the pork.
3. Lay the pork out on top of the vegetables in the crock pot and pour the beef broth over all.
4. Cover the crock pot and cook on low for 8-9 hours.
5. Slice the pork and serve with the vegetables and juices.

Note: If you have a hotter cooking crock pot, cook on low for 6-7 hours until pork registers 145 °F.

BEEF CHILI WITH PINTO BEANS

SERVINGS: 6-8 | PREP TIME: 20 min. | COOK TIME: 5 h.

CARBS: 14 g | FAT: 11 g | PROTEIN: 16 g | CALORIES: 220

INGREDIENTS

- 2 lb ground beef, 85% lean, or use part ground pork
- 1 cup chopped onion
- 3 cloves garlic, minced
- 4 oz chopped green chili peppers
- 3 Tbsp minced jalapeño peppers
- 1 large can (28 oz) crushed tomatoes
- 1 can (14.5 oz) diced tomatoes
- 3 Tbsp tomato paste, about half of a 6-oz can
- 1 can (15 oz) pinto beans, drained
- 3 Tbsp chili powder
- 1 tsp granulated sugar, optional
- ¾ tsp ground cumin
- ½ tsp red pepper
- ½ tsp freshly ground black pepper
- 1 tsp salt or to taste

DIRECTIONS

1. In a large skillet pan, brown the ground beef with the onion until no longer pink and the onion is tender. Add garlic, the canned chili peppers and jalapeño peppers and cook for 3 minutes more, stirring.
2. Move to a crock pot and add the crushed tomatoes, diced tomatoes, tomato paste, pinto beans, chili powder, sugar, cumin, red and black pepper, and salt, to taste.
3. Cover and cook on low for 5 to 6 hours or on high for 2 to 4 hours.
4. Serve with fresh baked buttermilk cornbread.

BROCCOLI & BEEF

SERVINGS: 4 | PREP TIME: 5 min. | COOK TIME: 6 h.

CARBS: 17 g | FAT: 32 g | PROTEIN: 156 g | CALORIES: 1034

INGREDIENTS

- 1½ lb beef steak, cut into thin stripes
- 14 oz broccoli florets
- 1 package (8 oz) Lee Kum Kee Sauce (Panda Sauce for Broccoli Beef)
- ¼ cup water
- Salt, pepper to taste

DIRECTIONS

1. Put the steak strips into the crockpot and pour in the water.
2. Close the lid. Cook for 2 hours on low.
3. Open the lid and drain the liquid from the crockpot. Pour Lee Kum Kee sauce over the beef, season with salt and pepper and add broccoli.
4. Close the lid and cook for 20 min on low.

SALSA CHICKEN

SERVINGS: 4 | PREP TIME: 5 min. | COOK TIME: 6 h.

CARBS: 3 g | FAT: 4 g | PROTEIN: 30 g | CALORIES: 176

INGREDIENTS

- *4 chicken breasts, boneless, skinless, halved*
- *2 cups salsa*
- *1 cup low-fat Mozzarella, grated*
- *1-2 Tbsp lemon juice*
- *Salt, pepper to taste*

DIRECTIONS

1. In a saucepan, simmer 2 cups of salsa until it is reduced to 1 cup.
2. Put the chicken in the crockpot in a single layer.
3. Season with salt, pepper.
4. Add lemon juice to salsa and pour the mixture over the chicken.
5. Cover and cook for 6 hours on high.
6. Open the lid and sprinkle the chicken with grated Mozzarella. Then cook for 5 min. or until the cheese melts.

CREAMY BEEF STROGANOFF

SERVINGS: 10 | PREP TIME: 25 min. | COOK TIME: 25 min.

CARBS: 37 g | FAT: 16 g | PROTEIN: 18 g | CALORIES: 360

INGREDIENTS

- *1 lb lean (at least 80%) ground beef*
- *2 packages (8 oz each) of sliced button mushrooms*
- *1 can (12 oz) evaporated milk*
- *1 lb uncooked medium egg noodles*
- *1 container (12 oz) of chive and onion sour cream*

DIRECTIONS

1. In a nonstick crock pot brown beef over high heat. Stir frequently.
2. Add mushrooms and salt to taste. Cook about 5 minutes.
3. Add 1 can milk, 4½ cups hot water and the noodles. Heat to boiling over high heat.
4. Reduce the heat and simmer uncovered for 7 to 8 minutes, stirring frequently. Remove from heat when the noodles are tender.

SMOTHERED CHICKEN

SERVINGS: 6 | PREP TIME: 10 min. | COOK TIME: 3 h. 10 min.

CARBS: 45 g | FAT: 23 g | PROTEIN: 35 g | CALORIES: 530

INGREDIENTS

- *1 package (20 oz) boneless, skinless chicken thighs (about 6)*
- *¼ cup chicken broth*
- *1 container (8 oz) of chive and onion cream cheese spread*
- *¼ tsp salt*
- *½ tsp pepper*
- *8 oz chopped cooked bacon*
- *1 cup frozen sweet peas*
- *cooked egg noodles, as desired*

DIRECTIONS

1. Spray the bottom of a 3-4 quart crock pot with cooking spray. Add chicken thighs.
2. In a small microwavable bowl, mix chicken broth, cream cheese spread, salt and pepper. Microwave, uncovered for 1 minute, and then beat with a whisk until smooth. Pour this mixture on top of the chicken thighs. Cover and cook on low heat setting 3 to 3½ hours.
3. Check for doneness piercing the thickest part of the chicken. The juice of the chicken must be running clear.
4. Stir ¾ cup of the bacon and the frozen sweet peas into the chicken mixture and mix well.
5. Increase the heat to high and cook 10 to 15 minutes longer or until the peas are cooked.
6. Serve over the cooked egg noodles top with remaining ¼ cup bacon.

BEEF ENCHILADA CASSEROLE

SERVINGS: 4-6 | PREP TIME: 10 min. | COOK TIME: 4 h.

CARBS: 32 g | FAT: 20 g | PROTEIN: 21 g | CALORIES: 400

INGREDIENTS

- 1½ pounds lean ground beef
- 1 cup chopped onion
- 1 can (10¾ oz) condensed cream of mushroom soup
- 1 can (10¾ oz) condensed cream of chicken soup
- 1 can (4 oz) diced green chilies
- 1 Tbsp chili powder
- ½ tsp ground cumin
- 1 can (15 oz) pinto beans, drained
- ⅓ cup water
- 1½ to 2 cups shredded Cheddar or Jack cheese, or combination
- 10 to 12 corn tortillas
- salsa, sour cream, sliced green onions, cilantro, or guacamole, for garnish.

DIRECTIONS

1. In a large skillet over medium heat, cook the ground beef with the chopped onions, stirring, until the beef is no longer pink.
2. Drain the ground beef and discard excess grease. To the ground beef add the two condensed soups, the diced green chile peppers, chili powder, cumin, drained pinto beans, and water. Mix to blend thoroughly.
3. Spoon some of the ground beef and bean mixture into the bottom of a crock pot.
4. Layer with some tortillas and then add more ground beef mixture, shredded cheese, and tortillas. Repeat layers until all of the ingredients are used. Amounts and the number of layers might vary depending on the size or dimensions of your crock pot.
5. Cover and cook on low for 4 hours.

FRENCH ONION CHICKEN

SERVINGS: 4 | PREP TIME: 25 min. | COOK TIME: 3 h. 20 min.

CARBS: 26 g | FAT: 21 g | PROTEIN: 44 g | CALORIES: 470

INGREDIENTS

- ¼ cup butter
- 2 sweet onions, thinly sliced
- 1 tsp salt
- ½ tsp pepper
- 1 tsp chopped fresh thyme
- 4 boneless, skinless chicken breasts, cut into small pieces
- 3 tsp cornstarch
- 2 tsp water
- 12 slices baguette, ½ inch thick (from 14-oz loaf)
- ½ cup shredded Swiss cheese (2 oz)

DIRECTIONS

1. In a nonstick skillet pan, melt butter over medium heat. Add onions, salt, pepper, and thyme cook 8 to 10 minutes, stirring occasionally, until onions are soft and golden brown.
2. Spoon onions into a 3½- to 4-quart crock pot. Stir in chicken. Cover and cook on low heat setting 2 to 3 hours or until chicken is no longer pink in center.
3. In a separate bowl, blend cornstarch with water. Stir into chicken mixture. Cover and cook on high heat setting 5 to 8 minutes or until thickened.
4. Meanwhile, set oven control to broil. Line a cookie sheet with foil. Arrange baguette slices in single layer on the cookie sheet. Top baguette slices with cheese. Broil above the heat until cheese is melted and edges are golden brown.
5. Serve with chicken.

COLORFUL STUFFED PEPPERS WITH GROUND BEEF AND RICE

SERVINGS: 6 | PREP TIME: 25 min. | COOK TIME: 1 h. 25 min.

CARBS: 23 g | FAT: 12 g | PROTEIN: 20 g | CALORIES: 267

INGREDIENTS

- 6 green or red bell peppers
- 1 Tbsp butter
- 1 Tbsp extra virgin olive oil
- ½ cup chopped onion
- ½ cup chopped celery
- 1 can (14.5 oz) diced tomatoes, undrained
- 1 can (8 ounces) tomato sauce
- 1 clove garlic, crushed
- 1 tsp dried oregano
- ½ tsp dried basil
- 2 tsp salt, divided
- ½ tsp ground black pepper, divided
- 1 egg, lightly beaten
- 1½ tsp Worcestershire sauce
- 1½ lb lean ground beef (at least 85%)
- 1½ cups cooked long-grain rice
- shredded mild Cheddar cheese, about ½ to ¾ cup, optional

DIRECTIONS

1. Cut the tops of the peppers off and remove seeds and pith.
2. Place the peppers into a large pot with salted water (enough to cover the peppers).
3. Boil, then reduce heat, cover, and simmer for 5 minutes.
4. In a large preheated with olive oil skillet pan sauté the chopped bell pepper from the tops, chopped onion, and chopped celery until the vegetables are tender.
5. Add the (undrained) can of diced tomatoes, tomato sauce, crushed garlic, oregano, basil, 1 tsp salt, and ¼ tsp of black pepper.
6. Simmer for about 10 minutes.
7. In a separate mixing bowl, combine an egg with the remaining 1 tsp of salt, ¼ tsp of black pepper, and Worcestershire sauce. Gently stir to blend. Add the ground beef, cooked rice, and 1 cup of the tomato sauce mixture. Mix well.
8. Heat a crock pot to 350° F.
9. Stuff the ground beef mixture into the peppers and place them in a baking pan.
10. Pour the remaining tomato mixture over the stuffed peppers.
11. Bake the peppers for about 45 minutes. You can use an instant-read thermometer to check the internal temperature (it should be at least 160° F for ground beef, pork or lamb, or 165° F for ground turkey or chicken).

BEEF ROAST & CARROTS

SERVINGS: 6 | PREP TIME: 5 min. | COOK TIME: 8 h.

CARBS: 2 g | FAT: 50 g | PROTEIN: 122 g | CALORIES: 972

INGREDIENTS

- *2 lb beef shoulder roast, boneless*
- *1-2 lb carrots, peeled, chopped*
- *3 Tbsp olive oil*
- *3 Tbsp chipotle seasoning*
- *Salt, pepper to taste*

DIRECTIONS

1. Combine all the ingredients in a crockpot.
2. Close the lid and cook for 8 hours on low.

MUSTARD CHICKEN FILLETS

SERVINGS: 6 | PREP TIME: 5 min. | COOK TIME: 6 h.

CARBS: 6 g | FAT: 9 g | PROTEIN: 18 g | CALORIES: 146

INGREDIENTS

- *6 chicken fillets, skinless, halved*
- *¼ cup chicken broth*
- *⅓ cup mustard, whole grain*
- *¼ cup yacón syrup*
- *Salt, pepper to taste*

DIRECTIONS

1. In a medium bowl mix mustard together with syrup and chicken broth.
2. Place the fillets into the crockpot.
3. Pour the mustard mixture over the chicken, flavor with salt and pepper.
4. Close the lid. Cook for 6 hours on low.

SOUTHWEST CHICKEN

SERVINGS: 6 | PREP TIME: 15 min. | COOK TIME: 6 h.

CARBS: 3 g | FAT: 2 g | PROTEIN: 19 g | CALORIES: 109

INGREDIENTS

- *4 chicken breasts, with boneless, skinless, halved*
- *1 zucchini, chopped*
- *1 bell pepper, cubed*
- *1 jar salsa, sugar free*
- *Salt, pepper to taste*

DIRECTIONS

1. In a large bowl stir the chicken breasts in salsa.
2. Put all the ingredients into the crockpot. Flavor with salt and pepper.
3. Close the lid. Cook for 6 hours on low.

HAWAIIAN CHICKEN

CARBS: 8 g | FAT: 17 g | PROTEIN: 39 g | CALORIES: 375

INGREDIENTS

- *6 chicken thighs, boneless*
- *8 bacon slices, 2 fried and crumbled for garnish*
- *½ cup red onion, cut in chunks*
- *1 cup fresh pineapple, sliced*
- *Salt, pepper to taste*

DIRECTIONS

1. In a skillet, fry 3 bacon slices until crisp.
2. Flavor the chicken with salt and pepper and place into the crockpot. Top with the uncooked bacon.
3. Lay onions and pineapple on top.
4. Close the lid. Cook for 6 hours on low.
5. Serve with fried crisp bacon.

MOIST TURKEY BREASTS

SERVINGS: 12 | PREP TIME: 15 min. | COOK TIME: 6 h.

CARBS: 2 g | FAT: 12 g | PROTEIN: 47 g | CALORIES: 318

INGREDIENTS

- *7 lb turkey breasts, no bones*
- *4 cloves garlic, sliced*
- *½ cup water*
- *1 Tbsp yacón syrup*
- *Salt, pepper to taste*

DIRECTIONS

1. Put all the ingredients into the crockpot.
2. Make sure all turkey pieces are evenly coated.
3. Cook for 6 hours on low.

GARLIC PARMESAN CHICKEN

SERVINGS: 6 | PREP TIME: 15 min. | COOK TIME: 6 h.

CARBS: 1 g | FAT: 34 g | PROTEIN: 28 g | CALORIES: 440

INGREDIENTS

- *2 lb chicken thighs, bone in*
- *1 cup Parmesan cheese, grated*
- *⅓ cup olive oil*
- *5 garlic cloves, chopped*
- *Seasoning: salt, pepper, thyme to taste*

DIRECTIONS

1. In a skillet heat ⅓ cup olive oil and brown chicken on both sides, for 2-3 min each side.
2. Add chicken to a crockpot and season with salt, pepper, garlic and thyme.
3. Close the lid and cook for 6 hours on low.
4. Open the lid, sprinkle with Parmesan and let sit for 15 min.

LIME PORK

SERVINGS: 6 | PREP TIME: 15 min. | COOK TIME: 6 h.

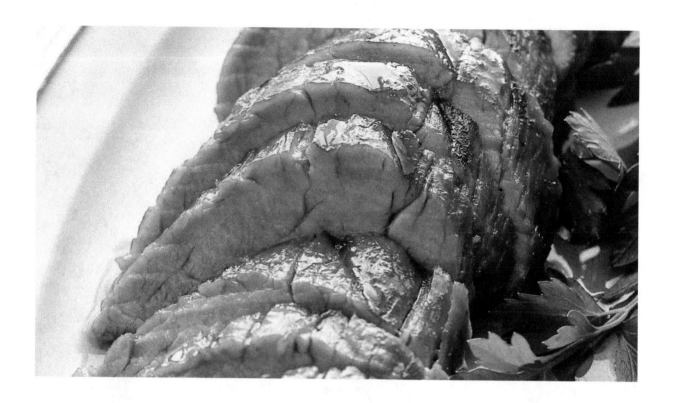

CARBS: 2 g | FAT: 14 g | PROTEIN: 19 g | CALORIES: 208

INGREDIENTS

- *3 lb pork sirloin chops, bone in*
- *5 Tbsp lime juice*
- *3 Tbsp olive oil*
- *½ tsp ground cumin*
- *Salt, pepper, parsley, garlic (minced fresh) to taste*

DIRECTIONS

1. In a large bowl mix the spices and stir the pork chops in the spice mixture to cover well.
2. Brown the chops on both sides in the olive oil in a frying pan for 5 min.
3. Put the chops into the crockpot and pour over the lime juice.
4. Close the lid and cook for 6 hours on high.

FIVE-SPICE CHICKEN WINGS

SERVINGS: 4 | PREP TIME: 15 min. | COOK TIME: 6 h.

CARBS: 3 g | FAT: 37 g | PROTEIN: 48 g | CALORIES: 532

INGREDIENTS

- *16 chicken wings*
- *2 Tbsp avocado oil (or your choice)*
- *2 Tbsp Chinese five-spice powder*
- *1 jalapenño, sliced*
- *Salt, pepper to taste*

DIRECTIONS

1. In a large bowl mix the wings with the oil, five-spice powder, salt and pepper.
2. Put the chicken wings into the crockpot.
3. Cook for 6 hours on low.
4. Top with jalapeño and serve over rice.

BARBECUED BLACK AND WHITE BEANS

SERVINGS: 12 | PREP TIME: 20 min. | COOK TIME: 3-4 h.

CARBS: 51 g | FAT: 3 g | PROTEIN: 13 g | CALORIES: 290

INGREDIENTS

- ½ lb bacon, cut into ½-inch pieces
- 1 medium onion, chopped (½ cup)
- 1 cup ketchup
- ½ cup packed brown sugar
- ¼ cup mild-flavor (light) molasses
- 1 Tbsp cider vinegar
- 1 tsp mustard powder
- 2 cans great northern beans, drained, rinsed
- 2 cans black beans, drained,
- ½ cup liquid reserved

DIRECTIONS

1. In a 10-inch skillet, cook bacon and onion over medium heat, stirring occasionally, until bacon is crisp and onions are tender drain.
2. In a 3½- to 4-quart crock pot, mix bacon, onion and remaining ingredients, including reserved liquid.
3. Cover and cook on low heat for 3 to 4 hours.

TOMATO SOUP

SERVINGS: 6-8 | PREP TIME: 5 min. | COOK TIME: 8 h.

CARBS: 10 g | FAT: 10 g | PROTEIN: 6 g | CALORIES: 145

INGREDIENTS

- *7 large ripe tomatoes*
- *½ cup raw macadamia nuts*
- *4 cups water or vegetable broth*
- *1 medium onion, chopped*
- *Seasoning: salt, pepper, basil to taste*

DIRECTIONS

1. In a nonstick skillet brown onions for 5 min.
2. Add all ingredients to a crockpot. Cook for 6-8 hours on low.
3. Using a blender make a smooth purée. Serve warm.

ZUCCHINI SOUP

SERVINGS: 4 | PREP TIME: 5 min. | COOK TIME: 8 h.

CARBS: 10 g | FAT: 1 g | PROTEIN: 4 g | CALORIES: 60

INGREDIENTS

- *3 zucchini, cut in chunks*
- *4 cups vegetable broth*
- *2 Tbsp low fat sour cream*
- *2 cloves garlic, minced*
- *Seasoning: salt, pepper, thyme, basil to taste*

DIRECTIONS

1. Combine all ingredients except sour cream in a crockpot
2. Close the lid. Cook for 6-8 hours on low.
3. Add sour cream and using a blender make a smooth purée.
4. Serve hot with Parmesan cheese if desired.

PUMPKIN SOUP

SERVINGS: 4 | PREP TIME: 5 min. | COOK TIME: 8 h.

CARBS: 9 g | FAT: 0.5 g | PROTEIN: 3 g | CALORIES: 58

INGREDIENTS

- *1 small pumpkin, halved, peeled, seeds removed, pulp cubed*
- *2 cups chicken broth*
- *1 cup coconut milk*
- *Seasonings: salt, pepper, ginger, cinnamon, nutmeg, garlic powder to taste*

DIRECTIONS

1. Combine all ingredients in the crockpot
2. Close the lid. Cook for 6-8 hours on low.
3. Using a blender make a smooth purée.
4. Decorate with roasted seeds and serve.

BUTTERNUT SQUASH AND SAGE BEEF STEW

SERVINGS: 5-6 | PREP TIME: 20 min. | COOK TIME: 8 h.

CARBS: 46 g | FAT: 11 g | PROTEIN: 56 g | CALORIES: 499

INGREDIENTS

- *2 lb beef stew meat*
- *½ lb bacon, diced*
- *2 cups butternut squash, diced*
- *1 cup button mushrooms*
- *½ yellow onion, minced*
- *3 garlic cloves, minced*
- *½ tsp garlic powder*
- *½ tsp salt*
- *8-10 sage leaves, minced*
- *bouquet of herbs (rosemary, thyme, and sage) tied in a cheesecloth bag.*
- *1 qt beef bone broth*
- *½ cup red wine*

DIRECTIONS

1. In a large sauté pan cook the bacon until crispy over medium heat. Remove and set aside.
2. Add the meat to the hot pan with the bacon grease, and sprinkle with garlic powder and salt. Brown on all sides for about 8 minutes. Set aside.
3. Add sage, onion and garlic to the pan and let sweat until the onions are translucent.
4. Add the mixture to a crock pot along with all the other ingredients and mix to combine.
5. Cover and cook for 8 hours on low. Remove herb bundle before serving.

TURKEY SPINACH SOUP

SERVINGS: 4 | PREP TIME: 5 min. | COOK TIME: 6 h.

CARBS: 10 g | FAT: 12 g | PROTEIN: 40 g | CALORIES: 347

INGREDIENTS

- *6 cups turkey stock*
- *2 cups boiled turkey meat, cubed*
- *4 cups fresh spinach, chopped*
- *1 Tbsp ginger and garlic mixture, half of each*
- *Salt, pepper to taste*

DIRECTIONS

1. Put all the ingredients into the crockpot. Close the lid and cook for 6 hours on low.
2. When done you can either serve it as is or use a blender to make a puréed soup.
3. Serve hot with toast.

MEXICAN CHICKEN SOUP

SERVINGS: 4 | PREP TIME: 5 min. | COOK TIME: 8 h.

CARBS: 7 g | FAT: 23 g | PROTEIN: 38 g | CALORIES: 400

INGREDIENTS

- 1½ lb skinless, boneless, chicken pieces
- 2 cups chicken broth
- 8 oz Pepper Jack cheese, cubed
- 15 oz chunky salsa

DIRECTIONS

1. Put the chicken pieces on the bottom of a crockpot.
2. Add remaining ingredients.
3. Cook for 8 hours on low.
4. Remove chicken pieces and shred, return to the pot.
5. Serve hot.

BROCCOLI CHEESE SOUP

SERVINGS: 6 | PREP TIME: 5 min. | COOK TIME: 6 h.

CARBS: 5 g | FAT: 25 g | PROTEIN: 13 g | CALORIES: 291

INGREDIENTS

- *4 cups broccoli, cut into florets*
- *3½ cups chicken broth*
- *1 cup heavy cream*
- *3 cups Cheddar cheese, shredded*
- *Seasoning: salt, pepper, bay leaves, garlic to taste*

DIRECTIONS

1. Add all ingredients except Cheddar into a crockpot. Close the lid and cook for 6 hours on low.
2. Open the lid and add the cheese. Cook for 15 min on high with the lid closed.
3. Remove the bay leaves and using a blender make a smooth purée and serve hot.

CREAM OF MUSHROOM SOUP

SERVINGS: 4 | PREP TIME: 5 min. | COOK TIME: 6 h.

CARBS: 8 g | FAT: 21 g | PROTEIN: 5 g | CALORIES: 229

INGREDIENTS

- *20 oz mushrooms, sliced*
- *2 cups chicken broth*
- *1 cup heavy cream*
- *1 cup almond milk, unsweetened*
- *Seasoning: salt, pepper, garlic, onion powder to taste*

DIRECTIONS

1. Add all ingredients to a crockpot. Close the lid and cook for 6 hours on low.
2. Using a blender purée until smooth and serve hot.

THAI CHICKEN SOUP

SERVINGS: 4 | PREP TIME: 5 min. | COOK TIME: 8 h.

CARBS: 10 g | FAT: 1 g | PROTEIN: 35 g | CALORIES: 63

INGREDIENTS

- *10 oz boneless, skinless chicken breasts, sliced*
- *7 oz mushrooms, sliced*
- *2-3 tomatoes, sliced*
- *4 cups water*
- *2 Tbsp tom yum paste*

DIRECTIONS

1. Into a crockpot add water, tom yum paste and chicken breasts.
2. Close the lid and cook for 4 hours on low.
3. Add mushrooms and tomatoes. Close the lid. Cook for another hour.

CHICKEN BROTH WITH CHICKEN & VEGETABLES

SERVINGS: 6-8 | PREP TIME: 5 min. | COOK TIME: 8 h.

CARBS: 5 g | FAT: 3 g | PROTEIN: 4 g | CALORIES: 53

INGREDIENTS

- *1 whole chicken, separated into pieces*
- *10 cups water*
- *2 carrots, peeled, cut into chunks*
- *1 onion, chopped*
- *Seasoning: salt, pepper, thyme, rosemary to taste*

DIRECTIONS

1. In a nonstick skillet brown onions for 5-7 min.
2. Add water to the crockpot and put in the chicken separated by wings, breast, legs and thighs.
3. Add carrots, onion and seasonings to the crockpot.
4. Close the lid and cook for 8 hours on low.

CAULIFLOWER SOUP

SERVINGS: 4 | PREP TIME: 5 min. | COOK TIME: 4 h. 15 min.

CARBS: 11 g | FAT: 8 g | PROTEIN: 10 g | CALORIES: 149

INGREDIENTS

- *1 cauliflower head, stalk removed, chopped*
- *4-5 cups chicken broth*
- *1 cup leeks, diced*
- *½ cup cream*
- *Salt, pepper to taste*

DIRECTIONS

1. Pour the broth into a crockpot, add chopped cauliflower and diced leeks, season with salt and pepper.
2. Close the lid and cook for 4 hours on low.
3. Open the lid and add the cream, cook with the lid open for 15 min. more.
4. Using a blender purée the soup and serve hot.

EGGPLANT AND TOMATO SAUCE WITH PASTA

SERVINGS: 6 | PREP TIME: 15 min. | COOK TIME: 4 h. 15 min.

CARBS: 76 g | FAT: 11 g | PROTEIN: 13 g | CALORIES: 360

INGREDIENTS

- *1 medium eggplant, cut into small cubes*
- *1 onion, finely chopped*
- *2 cloves garlic, finely chopped*
- *1 can (28 oz) Muir Glen Organic diced tomatoes, drained*
- *1 can (6 oz) tomato paste*
- *½ cup red wine or water*
- *1 tsp dried oregano*
- *½ tsp salt*
- *1 package (16 oz) rotini pasta*
- *shredded Parmesan cheese, if desired*

DIRECTIONS

1. Grease a crock pot with cooking spray. In the crock pot, mix all ingredients except pasta and cheese.
2. Cover and cook on low-heat setting for 4 hours or until eggplant is soft and sauce is thick.
3. Cook the pasta 15 minutes beforehand as directed on the package. Toss pasta with eggplant and tomato sauce.
4. Garnish individual servings with cheese.

WESTERN-STYLE BAKED BEANS

SERVINGS: 32 | PREP TIME: 25 min. | COOK TIME: 3 h. 15 min.

CARBS: 49 g | FAT: 147 g | PROTEIN: 12 g | CALORIES: 186

INGREDIENTS

- *2 (28 oz) cans baked beans with pork*
- *1 lb ground beef*
- *1 lb bacon, cooked and crumbled*
- *½ lb cooked ham, chopped*
- *2 Tbsp minced onion*
- *¼ cup ketchup*
- *1 Tbsp chili powder*
- *¼ cup packed brown sugar*
- *1 Tbsp molasses*
- *¼ cup water (if needed)*
- *½ cup cooking oil*

DIRECTIONS

1. Using cooking oil preheat a large skillet pan.
2. Crumble the ground beef in it over medium-high heat.
3. Cook 5 to 10 minutes.
4. With the grease drained off transfer the beef to a 4-quart or larger crock pot.
5. Stir in the baked beans, bacon, ham, onion, chili powder, ketchup, brown sugar and molasses. If it seems too thick, stir in the water.
6. Cover and cook on high for 3 hours or cook for 6 to 8 hours on low.

CREAMED CORN

SERVINGS: 12 | PREP TIME: 10 min. | COOK TIME: 4 h.

CARBS: 54 g | FAT: 38 g | PROTEIN: 14 g | CALORIES: 192

INGREDIENTS

- *20 oz. frozen corn kernels from two 16 oz packages*
- *1 (8 ounce) package cream cheese*
- *½ cup butter*
- *½ cup milk*
- *1 Tbsp white sugar*
- *salt and pepper to taste*

DIRECTIONS

1. In a crock pot, combine corn, cream cheese, butter, milk, and sugar.
2. Season with salt and pepper to taste.
3. Cook on high for 2 to 4 hours, or on low for 4 to 6 hours.

MAC AND CHEESE WITH CRUMBS

SERVINGS: 8 | PREP TIME: 20 min. | COOK TIME: 3 h. 20 min.

CARBS: 69 g | FAT: 48 g | PROTEIN: 37 g | CALORIES: 848

INGREDIENTS

- *3½ cups whole milk*
- *1 can (12 oz) evaporated milk*
- *1 box (16 oz) elbow macaroni*
- *4 cups shredded Cheddar cheese (16 oz)*
- *8 oz Kraft Velveeta cheese, cut into small cubes*
- *½ cup shredded Parmesan cheese*
- *2 Tbsp butter*
- *½ cup butter, melted*
- *1 tsp Dijon mustard*
- *¾ tsp salt*
- *¼ tsp black pepper*
- *⅛ tsp ground cayenne pepper*
- *⅔ cup crispy bread crumbs*

DIRECTIONS

1. Spray a crock pot with cooking spray. Beat the two milks, melted butter, mustard, salt, black pepper and cayenne pepper with a whisk.
2. Bring macaroni and 3½ cups of the Cheddar cheese, the cubed Velveeta cheese and the Parmesan cheese into a pot.
3. Cover and cook on low heat for one hour. Stir well. Cover again and cook 1 to 1½ hours longer. The pasta must not be mushy.
4. Stir until mac and cheese is creamy. Top with the remaining ½ cup Cheddar. Cover and leave to rest until the cheese is melted.
5. Meanwhile, in a 8-inch skillet pan, heat 2 tablespoons butter over medium heat. Add bread crumbs stir to coat. Cook and stir about 3 minutes.
6. Sprinkle over mac and cheese, and serve.

GARLIC MASHED POTATOES

SERVINGS: 14 | PREP TIME: 15 min. | COOK TIME: 4 h. 5 min.

CARBS: 21 g | FAT: 5 g | PROTEIN: 3 g | CALORIES: 140

INGREDIENTS

- *3 lb small red potatoes*
- *4 cloves garlic, finely chopped*
- *2 Tbsp olive oil*
- *1 tsp salt*
- *½ cup water*
- *½ cup of chives and onion cream cheese (from 8 oz container)*
- *¼ to ½ cup milk*

DIRECTIONS

1. Halve or quarter the potatoes as necessary to make similar-sized pieces. Place in a 4- to 6-quart crock pot.
2. Add garlic, oil, and salted water. Toss together making sure all potato pieces are coated.
3. Cover and cook on high setting 3½ to 4 ½ hours or until potatoes are tender.
4. Using any electric beater mash potatoes and garlic. Blend cream cheese and milk into potatoes for soft consistency.
5. Serve immediately, or cover and hold in the crock pot on low setting up to 2 hours.

FRIED RICE WITH EDAMAME BEANS

SERVINGS: 6 | PREP TIME: 10 min. | COOK TIME: 2 h.

CARBS: 56 g | FAT: 7 g | PROTEIN: 9 g | CALORIES: 320

INGREDIENTS

- *2 cups jasmine rice (dry white)*
- *½ cup frozen peas*
- *½ cup frozen carrots (diced)*
- *½ cup frozen edamame beans*
- *½ cup frozen, roasted corn*
- *2 whisked eggs*
- *1 tsp shallots, minced*
- *2 Tbsp salted butter*
- *1 tsp ground pepper (fresh)*
- *2 tsp low sodium soy sauce*
- *2 tsp Worcestershire sauce*

DIRECTIONS

1. Add 4 cups of water to a crock pot.
2. Add all stirred ingredients to the crock pot.
3. Close lid and let cook for 1½ to 2 hours on high.

SPANISH RICE GOLDEN BROWN

SERVINGS: 4 | PREP TIME: 20 min. | COOK TIME: 2 h. 20 min.

CARBS: 5 g | FAT: 4 g | PROTEIN: 1 g | CALORIES: 55

INGREDIENTS

- 2 Tbsp olive oil, plus more for the crock pot
- 2 cups raw white rice, such as jasmine
- 1 medium yellow onion, chopped
- 1 (14.5 oz) can diced tomatoes
- 3 cloves garlic, minced
- ½ red bell pepper, medium, diced
- ½ yellow bell pepper, medium, diced
- 2 cups low-sodium broth or stock (chicken or vegetable), or water
- 2 tsp chili powder
- 1½ tsp ground cumin
- 1½ tsp salt
- 2 Tbsp fresh cilantro leaves, for garnishing

DIRECTIONS

1. Add the raw rice into a preheated with olive oil skillet pan.
2. Sauté with onion, stirring constantly, until the rice turns a pale golden brown, about 5 minutes.
3. Lightly coat the bottom and sides of a crock pot with olive oil. Bring the browned rice to the crock pot, along with the tomatoes, garlic, bell peppers, chili powder, cumin, broth and salt.
4. Stir and cook on high for 2 hours 20 minutes the lid covered. Cook until all the liquid is absorbed and the rice is tender.
5. Garnish with cilantro and serve.

STUFFED PEPPERS

SERVINGS: 4 | PREP TIME: 5 min. | COOK TIME: 6 h.

CARBS: 10 g | FAT: 11 g | PROTEIN: 107 g | CALORIES: 558

INGREDIENTS

- *1 lb ground turkey*
- *4 bell peppers, tops and seeds removed*
- *1 onion, diced*
- *1 jar (24 oz) tomato sauce*
- *Salt, pepper to taste*

DIRECTIONS

1. In a large bowl combine the ground meat, onion and 2 Tbsp of pasta sauce.
2. Stuff the peppers firmly.
3. Put the peppers into a crockpot and cover with the remaining pasta sauce.
4. Cover and cook for 6 hours on low.

BACON-FLAVORED CABBAGE

SERVINGS: 8 | PREP TIME: 10 min. | COOK TIME: 6 h.

CARBS: 12 g | FAT: 6 g | PROTEIN: 9 g | CALORIES: 138

INGREDIENTS

- *1 small head of cabbage, cored, chopped*
- *⅔ cup cooked, crumbled bacon*
- *15 oz pearl onions,*
- *8 cups chicken broth*
- *Salt, pepper to taste*

DIRECTIONS

1. Place the chopped cabbage into a crockpot.
2. Top with onions and bacon. Season with salt and pepper.
3. Pour the broth over the cabbage.
4. Close the lid and cook for 6 hours on high.

YELLOW SQUASH CASSEROLE

SERVINGS: 8 | PREP TIME: 10 min. | COOK TIME: 6 h.

CARBS: 6 g | FAT: 5 g | PROTEIN: 5 g | CALORIES: 97

INGREDIENTS

- *2 lb yellow squash, sliced across*
- *1 cup chopped onion*
- *2 cups salted crackers , crumbled*
- *1 cup Cheddar cheese, shredded*
- *1 Tbsp butter*

DIRECTIONS

1. Microwave squash, onion and 1 tablespoon butter for 10 minutes uncovered.
2. Add the squash mixture together with ½ cup cheese and 1 cup cracker crumbs into a crockpot.
3. In a separate bowl combine the remaining cheese with 1 cup of cracker crumbs, and sprinkle over the squash.
4. Close the lid and cook for 2 hours on low.
5. Turn the heat off and let stand for 30 min

GARLICKY MEATBALL BISCUITS WITH CHEESE

SERVINGS: 4 | PREP TIME: 15 min. | COOK TIME: 25 min.

CARBS: 16 g | FAT: 3 g | PROTEIN: 3.5 g | CALORIES: 105

INGREDIENTS

- *12 oz. can of any frozen flaky biscuits*
- *frozen cooked meatballs, 10 pcs.*
- *string cheese, 2 sticks*
- *Parmesan cheese, grated*
- *Italian seasoning, 1 Tbsp*
- *garlic powder, 1 tsp*

DIRECTIONS

1. Heat a crock pot to 375 °F. Split the 10 biscuits and cut each meatball in half.
2. Slice each stick of string cheese into 10 pieces.
3. Place one meatball half into a biscuit half, add the string cheese piece.
4. Make the balls out of the biscuits, the dough covering the meat and the cheese.
5. Place all 20 meatballs in an ungreased round cake pan.
6. Sprinkle with the Parmesan cheese, Italian seasoning and garlic powder to your liking.
7. Cook for 25 minutes.

EGGPLANT PARMIGIANA

SERVINGS: 6-8 | PREP TIME: 15 min. | COOK TIME: 5 h.

CARBS: 51 g | FAT: 13 g | PROTEIN: 13 g | CALORIES: 353

INGREDIENTS

- *3 medium eggplants, peeled, cut in 2 inch slices*
- *⅓ cup seasoned bread crumbs*
- *½ cup Parmesan, grated*
- *32 oz marinara sauce*
- *Salt, pepper to taste*

DIRECTIONS

1. Using olive oil, sauté the eggplants in a large skillet until lightly brown.
2. In a separate bowl combine the seasoned bread crumbs with grated Parmesan.
3. Layer the eggplants into a crockpot beginning with eggplant, next top with crumbs, then marinara sauce. Repeat layers.
4. Close the lid and cook for 5 hours on low.

CHIPOTLE RANCH CHICKEN PIZZA

SERVINGS: 8 | PREP TIME: 10 min. | COOK TIME: 20 min.

CARBS: 22 g | FAT: 20 g | PROTEIN: 16 g | CALORIES: 330

INGREDIENTS

- *2 cups Bisquick mix*
- *8 oz pepper Jack cheese, shredded*
- *½ cup hot water*
- *⅓ cup chipotle ranch dressing*
- *5 Tbsp fresh cilantro, chopped*
- *1½ cups deli rotisserie chicken, shredded*
- *1 cup tomato, chopped*

DIRECTIONS

1. Heat a crock pot to 400 ° F. Grease a pizza pan with cooking spray.
2. In a separate bowl stir Bisquick mix, ¾ cup of the cheese and the hot water with a spoon until soft dough forms. Press dough evenly in the pizza pan.
3. Bake for 8 minutes in the crock pot. Spread dressing evenly over partially baked crust. Sprinkle 4 Tbsp of the cilantro and ¾ cup of the cheese on the dressing. Layer the chicken, tomato and remaining cheese.
4. Bake until the edges of the crust are golden brown. Sprinkle with remaining fresh cilantro.

SWEET AND SOUR SMOKED SAUSAGE

SERVINGS: 4 | PREP TIME: 10 min. | COOK TIME: 4 h.

CARBS: 82 g | FAT: 33 g | PROTEIN: 17 g | CALORIES: 691

INGREDIENTS

- *2 lb smoked sausage*
- *2 cans (21 ounces each) cherry pie filling*
- *1 can (20 ounces) pineapple chunks, drained*
- *3 Tbsp brown sugar*

DIRECTIONS

1. Place sausages in a crockpot.
2. In a separate bowl combine the pie filling, pineapple and sugar.
3. Pour over the sausages.
4. Cover the lid and cook on low heat for 4 hours.

ARTICHOKE AND SPINACH HOMEMADE SAUCE

SERVINGS: 4 | PREP TIME: 10 min. | COOK TIME: 2-4 h.

CARBS: 5.5 g | FAT: 11 g | PROTEIN: 7.7 g | CALORIES: 150

INGREDIENTS

- *1 9 oz box of frozen spinach, thawed and squeezed to drain*
- *1 14 oz can quartered artichoke hearts, drained and chopped*
- *½ cup Alfredo sauce*
- *½ cup mayonnaise*
- *¾ tsp garlic salt*
- *¼ tsp pepper*
- *1 cup shredded Swiss cheese*

DIRECTIONS

1. Mix all ingredients in a large crock pot.
2. Cover and cook on low for 2 to 4 hours before serving.
3. Serve with crackers or toasted bread.

BUFFALO CHICKEN SAUCE

SERVINGS: 4 | PREP TIME: 10 min. | COOK TIME: 30 min.

CARBS: 0 g | FAT: 9 g | PROTEIN: 1.2 g | CALORIES: 100

INGREDIENTS

- 3 10 oz cans of chicken (drained)
- 2 8 oz packages of cream cheese (softened)
- 8 oz buffalo wing sauce
- 6 oz ranch or blue cheese dressing
- 2 cups Cheddar cheese

DIRECTIONS

1. Preheat a crock pot to 350 °F.
2. In a separate bowl mix all the ingredients shredding the chicken.
3. Put the dip mixture into a casserole dish and bake for 30 min.

PULLED CHICKEN SANDWICHES

SERVINGS: 8 | PREP TIME: 15 min. | COOK TIME: 8 h.

CARBS: 38 g | FAT: 12 g | PROTEIN: 32 g | CALORIES: 399

INGREDIENTS

- *nonstick cooking spray*
- *2 pounds boneless, skinless chicken thighs*
- *1 cup sliced onion*
- *¼ cup chopped jalapeño (or hot chili) peppers*
- *1 can (15 oz) Manwich Original Sloppy Joe Sauce*
- *¼ tsp salt*
- *8 Kaiser rolls*

DIRECTIONS

1. Spray the inside of a 4-quart crock pot with cooking spray. Place chicken, onion, jalapeño and Sloppy Joe sauce in the crock pot. Cook on low for 8 hours with the lid covered until the chicken is tender.
2. Transfer the chicken to a cutting board and shred it. Return the chicken to the crock pot. Sprinkle with salt and stir. Reduce heat. Serve on the rolls.

CANDIED NUTS

SERVINGS: 25 | PREP TIME: 20 min. | COOK TIME: 2 h.

CARBS: 16 g | FAT: 25 g | PROTEIN: 1 g | CALORIES: 73

INGREDIENTS

- *1 lb whole unsalted almonds*
- *1½ cups granulated sugar*
- *2 tsp cinnamon*
- *½ tsp sea salt*
- *2 egg whites*
- *¼ tsp vanilla extract*

DIRECTIONS

1. Combine dry ingredients with nuts in a bowl and mix. Set aside.
2. In a separate bowl, whisk the egg whites with vanilla extract until frothy.
3. Bring the nuts to the egg mixture and coat all the nuts.
4. Put the nut mixture into a crock pot that has been sprayed with cooking spray.
5. Cook on low for 2 hours, stirring every 30 minutes.
6. When done cooking, spread nuts on a baking sheet, lined with parchment paper, to cool.

CINNAMON GREEN APPLES

SERVINGS: 8 | PREP TIME: 15 min. | COOK TIME: 6 h.

CARBS: 48 g | FAT: 11 g | PROTEIN: 2 g | CALORIES: 280

INGREDIENTS

- *6 medium Granny Smith apples, peeled, cored, and cut into eighths*
- *1 Tbsp lemon juice*
- *½ cup packed dark brown sugar*
- *½ cup chopped walnuts*
- *½ cup maple-flavored syrup*
- *¼ cup sweetened dried cranberries*
- *¼ cup butter, melted*
- *2 tsp ground cinnamon*
- *2 Tbsp water*
- *1 Tbsp cornstarch*

DIRECTIONS

1. Grease a crock pot with cooking spray. Toss apples in the crock pot with lemon juice. Coat them with brown sugar, walnuts, syrup, cranberries, melted butter and cinnamon.
2. Cover and cook on low-heat setting for 3 hours.
3. In a small bowl, stir together water and cornstarch until smooth. Stir into apple mixture in the crock pot.
4. Cover and cook 3 hours longer or until apples are tender.

ORIENTAL SNACK MIX

SERVINGS: 28 | PREP TIME: 10 min. | COOK TIME: 1 h. 10 min.

CARBS: 12 g | FAT: 8 g | PROTEIN: 3 g | CALORIES: 130

INGREDIENTS

- *6 Tbsp butter or margarine*
- *1 tsp garlic powder*
- *2 Tbsp soy sauce*
- *1 package (1 oz) Chow Mein oriental mix*
- *4 cups Corn Chex cereal*
- *4 cups Bugles original corn snacks*
- *2 cups chow mein noodles*
- *1 cup pretzel sticks*
- *1 cup salted peanuts*
- *1 cup wasabi peas*

DIRECTIONS

1. Heat a crock pot to 250° F. In a 1-quart saucepan, melt butter over medium heat. Remove from heat. Add Chow Mein seasoning mix, garlic powder, and soy sauce with a wire whisk until well mixed.
2. Mix the remaining ingredients except wasabi peas. Pour butter mixture over the cereal mixture toss evenly to coat.
3. Bake 50 to 55 minutes, stirring every 15 minutes, until mixture looks dry and crisp. Pour mixture onto paper towels. Cool 15 minutes. Stir in wasabi peas before serving. Store in a tightly covered container.

CHOCOLATE-BUTTERSCOTCH LAVA CAKE

SERVINGS: 12 | PREP TIME: 15 min. | COOK TIME: 4 h. 45 min.

CARBS: 70 g | FAT: 25 g | PROTEIN: 8 g | CALORIES: 534

INGREDIENTS

- *1 box (4-serving size) chocolate instant pudding and pie filling mix*
- *1 box (4-serving size) butterscotch instant pudding and pie filling mix*
- *1 box dark chocolate cake mix*
- *1 cup sour cream*
- *⅓ cup butter or margarine, melted*
- *3 eggs*
- *3¼ cups milk*
- *1 bag (8 oz) toffee bits*
- *1 tsp vanilla extract*
- *8 oz frozen whipped topping, thawed*

DIRECTIONS

1. Spray a 5-quart oval crock pot with cooking spray. In a large bowl, using an electric mixer beat cake mix, chocolate pudding mix, sour cream, butter, 1¼ cups of the milk, the eggs and vanilla extract. Stir in 1 cup of the toffee bits. Pour batter into the crock pot.
2. In a 2-quart saucepan, heat remaining 2 cups milk over medium heat for 3 to 5 minutes, stirring frequently, until hot and bubbly. Remove from heat. Sprinkle butterscotch pudding mix over batter in the crock pot. Slowly pour hot milk over pudding.
3. Cover and cook on low-heat setting 4 hours 30 minutes or until edge of cake is set for at least 2 inches from the side of the crock pot but center still jiggles slightly when moved. Turn off the crock pot. Leave to rest for 15 minutes.
4. Serve with whipped topping and toffee bits.

PUMPKIN SWIRL CHEESECAKE

SERVINGS: 8 | PREP TIME: 20 min. | COOK TIME: 10 h.

CARBS: 41 g | FAT: 28 g | PROTEIN: 6 g | CALORIES: 440

INGREDIENTS

Cheesecake:
- 2 packages (8 oz each) cream cheese, softened
- 2 eggs
- ¾ cup sugar
- ½ cup canned pumpkin
- ½ tsp pumpkin pie spice

Crust:
- 1¼ cups graham cracker crumbs
- ⅓ cup sugar
- ¼ cup butter, melted

DIRECTIONS

1. Apply some cooking spray on a spring form pan. In a small bowl, mix crust ingredients. Form the crust at the bottom of the pan 1 inch up the sides.
2. In a large bowl, using an electric mixer beat cream cheese just until smooth.
3. Lower the speed and gradually beat in ¾ cup sugar, and then beat in the eggs, one at a time, just until blended.
4. Spread three-fourths of the cream cheese mixture into the pan.
5. Beat pumpkin and pumpkin pie spice into remaining cream cheese mixture with whisk until smooth. Spoon over mixture in pan.
6. Place a small ovenproof bowl on the bottom of a 6- or 7-quart round crock pot (about 9 inches in diameter). Place a heatproof plate on top of the bowl. Set the cheesecake on the plate. Place three layers of paper towels across the top of the crock pot. Cover it with the lid to seal. Cook on high- heat setting for 3 hours without removing the lid. Turn the crock pot off and let stand, untouched, one hour.
7. Open the lid and remove paper towels. Transfer the cheesecake to the refrigerator. Refrigerate before serving, not less 6 hours and no longer than 24.

TRIPLE CHOCOLATE-COVERED NUT CLUSTERS

SERVINGS: 60 | PREP TIME: 15 min. | COOK TIME: 2 h. 15 min.

CARBS: 21 g | FAT: 17 g | PROTEIN: 5 g | CALORIES: 244

INGREDIENTS

- *16 oz dry-roasted peanuts, salted*
- *16 oz dry-roasted peanuts, unsalted*
- *1 can (9.75 oz) whole cashews, salted*
- *36 oz chocolate-flavored candy coating, chopped*
- *12 oz (2 cups) semisweet chocolate chips*
- *1 bar (4 oz) sweet baking chocolate, chopped*
- *1 tsp vanilla extract*

DIRECTIONS

1. Spray a 3½- to 4-quart crock pot with cooking spray. In the crock pot, mix all ingredients except cashews and vanilla extract.
2. Cover and cook on low-heat setting for 2 hours.
3. Line the necessary number of cookie sheets (depending on their size) with waxed paper. Stir mixture in the crock pot until smooth. Add cashews and vanilla extract stir until cashews are coated. Drop mixture by heaping tablespoon onto cookie sheets. Let stand until firm. Store tightly covered at room temperature.

TROPICAL BANANAS FOSTER

SERVINGS: 7 | PREP TIME: 10 min. | COOK TIME: 1 h. 15 min.

CARBS: 45 g | FAT: 7 g | PROTEIN: 3 g | CALORIES: 260

INGREDIENTS

- *½ cup dark brown sugar*
- *3 Tbsp butter, cut into pieces*
- *¼ cup light unsweetened coconut milk*
- *1 cup fresh pineapples, cubed*
- *4 ripe bananas, cut into ½-inch-thick slices*
- *1¾ cups vanilla reduced-fat ice cream*
- *¼ tsp ground cinnamon*
- *¼ cup dark rum*

DIRECTIONS

1. Spray a 3½-quart crock pot with cooking spray. In the crock pot, stir together the brown sugar, butter, coconut milk and rum.
2. Cover and cook on low-heat setting for one hour.
3. Whisking makes a smooth mixture. Coat the pineapples, cinnamon and bananas in the sauce. Cover and cook 15 minutes longer.
4. Serve warm with ice cream.

PEACHES AND CREAM TAPIOCA

SERVINGS: 8 | PREP TIME: 10 min. | COOK TIME: 4 h.

CARBS: 52 g | FAT: 13 g | PROTEIN: 4 g | CALORIES: 330

INGREDIENTS

- *4 cups peaches, sliced (fresh or thawed from frozen)*
- *3 Tbsp quick-cooking tapioca*
- *¾ cup packed brown sugar*
- *⅛ tsp salt*
- *⅛ tsp ground nutmeg*
- *1 cup whipping cream*
- *½ cup peach nectar*
- *2 cups granola*
- *Whipped topping, if desired*

DIRECTIONS

1. Spray a 3½-quart crock pot with cooking spray. In the crock pot, stir together peaches, tapioca, brown sugar, salt, nutmeg, whipping cream and peach nectar.
2. Cover and cook on low-heat setting for 4 hours.
3. Stir well spoon into dessert dishes. Top each serving with whipped topping and ¼ cup granola.

PEACH-PLUM COBBLER

SERVINGS: 8 | PREP TIME: 20 min. | COOK TIME: 4 h. 15 min.

CARBS: 70 g | FAT: 13 g | PROTEIN: 5 g | CALORIES: 397

INGREDIENTS

- *1½ lb peaches, peeled, sliced*
- *1½ lb plums, sliced*
- *¾ cup granulated sugar*
- *4½ tsp cornstarch*
- *1½ tsp fresh lemon juice*
- *½ tsp almond extract*
- *½ cup milk*
- *¼ cup butter or margarine, melted*
- *2 Tbsp cinnamon sugar*
- *⅓ cup sliced almonds, toasted*

DIRECTIONS

1. Spray a 3½- to 4-quart crock pot with cooking spray. In a large bowl, mix peaches, plums, ½ cup of the granulated sugar, the cornstarch, lemon juice and almond extract. Transfer mixture to the crock pot.
2. In a separate bowl, blend together the remaining ¼ cup granulated sugar, the milk and the butter. Drop heaping tablespoon of dough into 8 mounds on the fruit in the crock pot.
3. Cover and cook on high-heat setting for 3 hours 30 minutes or until topping is dry in the center and the fruit is bubbly.
4. Sprinkle cinnamon sugar over topping. Cover and cook 30 minutes longer. Let stand 15 minutes before serving. Sprinkle with almonds.

BROWNIES

SERVINGS: 8 | PREP TIME: 5 min. | COOK TIME: 4 h.

CARBS: 33 g | FAT: 17 g | PROTEIN: 8 g | CALORIES: 202

INGREDIENTS

- *3 eggs*
- *1 cup almond butter*
- *10 Tbsp cocoa powder, unsweetened*
- *½ tsp baking powder*
- *¾ cup erythritol, powdered*

DIRECTIONS

1. Using a blender mix together almond butter and erythritol.
2. Beat in eggs, add cocoa and baking powders.
3. Cover the crockpot bottom with foil sheet. Spread the batter evenly and cook for 2 hours on low with the lid closed.
4. Let the brownies sit with the heat off for another 2 hours.

RASPBERRY COOKIES

SERVINGS: 8 | PREP TIME: 5 min. | COOK TIME: 4 h.

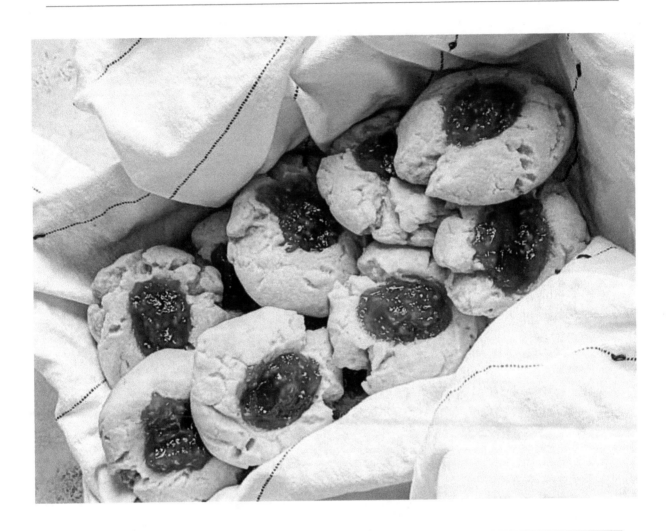

CARBS: 5 g | FAT: 7 g | PROTEIN: 2 g | CALORIES: 73

INGREDIENTS

- *1 egg*
- *1 cup almond flour*
- *4 oz cream cheese, softened*
- *1 oz raspberries*
- *6 Tbsp erythritol, powdered*

DIRECTIONS

1. Using a blender mix together 2 oz cheese cream, an egg, 4 Tbsp erythritol and flour.
2. To make the filling blend 2 oz cheese cream with 1 Tbsp erythritol. In a separate bowl blend 1 Tbsp erythritol with raspberries.
3. Cover the crockpot bottom with a foil sheet. Using a spoon scoop the batter onto it making small cookies. Make hollow in the center of each cookie and fill them with the cream cheese mixture followed by raspberries.
4. Close the lid and cook for 4 hours on low.

LEMON CAKE

CARBS: 9 g | FAT: 20 g | PROTEIN: 4 g | CALORIES: 200

INGREDIENTS

- *2 eggs*
- *2 cups almond flour*
- *Zest from 2 lemons*
- *½ cup melted butter*
- *6 Tbsp Swerve*

DIRECTIONS

1. In a medium bowl mix flour with sweetener.
2. In another bowl whisk together eggs, butter and lemon zest.
3. Combine dry and wet mixtures and blend well.
4. Cover the crockpot bottom with foil and spread the batter.
5. Close the lid and cook for 3 hours on high.

BEET CAKE

SERVINGS: 6-8 | PREP TIME: 15 min. | COOK TIME: 3 h.

CARBS: 11 g | FAT: 19 g | PROTEIN: 6 g | CALORIES: 224

INGREDIENTS

- *14 oz beets, cooked and peeled*
- *4 eggs*
- *⅔ cup cocoa powder*
- *½ cup honey*
- *½ cup vegetable oil*

DIRECTIONS

1. Cover the crockpot bottom with foil.
2. Purée the beets, stir in oil, honey, cocoa and eggs (one at a time).
3. Spread over the foil. Close the lid and cook for 3 hours on low.
4. Serve cool with grated chocolate.

VANILLA BEAN CUSTARD

SERVINGS: 4 | PREP TIME: 15 min. | COOK TIME: 1 h. 45 min.

CARBS: 27 g | FAT: 5 g | PROTEIN: 9 g | CALORIES: 190

INGREDIENTS

- *1 can (12 oz) evaporated low-fat milk*
- *½ cup 1% low-fat milk*
- *1 tsp vanilla bean paste*
- *1 whole egg*
- *2 egg yolks*
- *⅓ cup sugar*

DIRECTIONS

1. In a 2-quart saucepan, warm up the evaporated milk and the 1% milk to simmering over medium heat, about 4 minutes.
2. Remove from heat and whisk in vanilla bean paste.
3. In a medium bowl, beat the egg, egg yolks and sugar with a whisk until blended. Gradually add the hot milk mixture, stirring vigorously. Pour the egg mixture through a strainer into a separate bowl.
4. Place 4 metal canning jar bands in a 6-quart oval crock pot. Spoon egg mixture evenly into 4 (8-oz) individual baking dishes (ramekins). Cover dishes with foil. Place one dish on each band, making sure the dishes do not touch each other or the side of the crock pot. Carefully pour hot water into the crock pot to a depth of one inch up the sides of the dishes.
5. Cover and cook on high-heat setting for one hour 45 minutes. Check for doneness with a knife inserted in the center of the custards which must come out clean. Remove dishes from the crock pot to a cooling rack.
6. Serve warm or chilled.

CONCLUSION

Thank you for reading this book and having the patience to try the recipes.

I do hope that you have had as much enjoyment reading and experimenting with the meals as I have had writing the book.

Stay safe and healthy!

RECIPE INDEX

CONVERSION TABLES

Dry Weights

OZ	(spoon)	C (cup)	(scale)	(scale)
1/2 OZ	1 Tbsp	1/16 C	15 g	
1 OZ	2 Tbsp	1/8 C	28 g	
2 OZ	4 Tbsp	1/4 C	57 g	
3 OZ	6 Tbsp	1/3 C	85 g	
4 OZ	8 Tbsp	1/2 C	115 g	1/4 lb
8 OZ	16 Tbsp	1 C	227 g	1/2 lb
12 OZ	24 Tbsp	1 1/2 C	340 g	3/4 lb
16 OZ	32 Tbsp	2 C	455 g	1 lb

Liquid Conversions

1 Gallon:
4 quarts
8 pints
16 cups
128 fl oz
3.8 liters

1 Quart:
2 pints
4 cups
32 fl oz
0.95 liters

1 Pint:
2 cups
16 fl oz
480 ml

1 Cup:
16 Tbsp
8 fl oz
240 ml

OZ	(spoon)	(spoon)	mL	C	Pt	Qt
1 oz	6 tsp	2 Tbsp	30 ml	1/8 C		
2 oz	12 tsp	4 Tbsp	60 ml	1/4 C		
2 2/3 oz	16 tsp	5 Tbsp	80 ml	1/3 C		
4 oz	24 tsp	8 Tbsp	120 ml	1/2 C		
5 1/3 oz	32 tsp	11 Tbsp	160 ml	2/3 C		
6 oz	36 tsp	12 Tbsp	177 ml	3/4 C		
8 oz	48 tsp	16 Tbsp	237 ml	1 C	1/2 pt	1/4 qt
16 oz	96 tsp	32 Tbsp	480 ml	2 C	1 pt	1/2 qt
32 oz	192 tsp	64 Tbsp	950 ml	4 C	2 pt	1 qt

Fahrenheit to Celcius (F to C)

500 F = 260 C
475 F = 245 C
450 F = 235 C
425 F = 220 C
400 F = 205 C
375 F = 190 C
350 F = 180 C
325 F = 160 C
300 F = 150 C
275 F = 135 C
250 F = 120 C
225 F = 107 C

1 Tbsp: 15 ml

1 tsp: 5 ml

Safe Cooking Meat Temperatures

Minimum temperatures:

USDA Safe at 145 F

USDA Safe at 160 F

USDA Safe at 165 F

Beef Steaks, Briskets, and Roasts; Pork Chops, Roasts, Ribs, Shoulders, and Butts; Lamb Chops, Legs, and Roasts; Fresh Hams, Veal Steaks, Fish, and Shrimp

Ground Meats (except poultry)

Chicken & Turkey, ground or whole

Printed in the USA
CPSIA information can be obtained
at www.ICGtesting.com
LVHW081949271023
762373LV00013B/1441